L•Leonard
TRUMENTAL
LAY-ALONG

AUDIO
ACCESS
INCLUDED

AYBACK+
• Pitch • Balance • Loop

TROMBONE

SUPERHERO THEMES

Audio arrangements by Peter Deneff

To access audio, visit:
www.halleonard.com/mylibrary

Enter Code
5693-7973-3072-4631

ISBN 978-1-70513-164-0

HAL•LEONARD®

Visit Hal Leonard Online at
www.halleonard.com

Contact us:
Hal Leonard
7777 West Bluemound Road
Milwaukee, WI 53213
Email: info@halleonard.com

In Europe, contact:
Hal Leonard Europe Limited
42 Wigmore Street
Marylebone, London, W1U 2RN
Email: info@halleonardeurope.com

In Australia, contact:
Hal Leonard Australia Pty. Ltd.
4 Lentara Court
Cheltenham, Victoria, 3192 Australia
Email: info@halleonard.com.au

THEME FROM ANT-MAN

from MARVEL'S ANT-MAN

TROMBONE

Music by CHRISTOPHE BECK

WAKANDA

from BLACK PANTHER

Music by LUDWIG GÖRANSSON

THE AVENGERS
from THE AVENGERS

TROMBONE

Composed by
ALAN SILVESTRI

BATMAN THEME

TROMBONE

Words and Music by
NEAL HEFTI

CAPTAIN AMERICA MARCH
from CAPTAIN AMERICA

TROMBONE

By ALAN SILVESTRI

ELASTIGIRL IS BACK

from INCREDIBLES 2

TROMBONE

Composed by
MICHAEL GIACCHINO

IMMORTALS

from BIG HERO 6

TROMBONE

Words and Music by ANDREW HURLEY,
JOE TROHMAN, PATRICK STUMP
and PETE WENTZ

GUARDIANS INFERNO

from GUARDIANS OF THE GALAXY VOL. 2

TROMBONE

Words and Music by JAMES GUNN
and TYLER BATES

THE INCREDITS
from THE INCREDIBLES

TROMBONE

Music by MICHAEL GIACCHINO

POW! POW! POW! - MR. INCREDIBLES THEME

from INCREDIBLES 2

TROMBONE

Music and Lyrics by
MICHAEL GIACCHINO

IRON MAN
from IRON MAN

TROMBONE

By RAMIN DJAWADI

ROCKETEER END TITLES

from THE ROCKETEER

TROMBONE

By JAMES HORNER

THEME FROM SPIDER MAN

TROMBONE

Written by BOB HARRIS
and PAUL FRANCIS WEBSTER

X-MEN: APOCALYPSE - END TITLES

from X-MEN: APOCALYPSE

TROMBONE

By JOHN OTTMAN